# Hello, Little Love!

## A letter from a parent to their baby in the NICU

Written by

**Melissa Kirsch**

Illustrated by

**Christa Craycraft**

WestBow Press books may be ordered through booksellers or by contacting:

WestBow Press
A Division of Thomas Nelson & Zondervan
1663 Liberty Drive
Bloomington, IN 47403
www.westbowpress.com
844-714-3454

Because of the dynamic nature of the Internet, any web addresses or links contained in this book may have changed since publication and may no longer be valid. The views expressed in this work are solely those of the author and do not necessarily reflect the views of the publisher, and the publisher hereby disclaims any responsibility for them.

Any people depicted in stock imagery provided by Getty Images are models, and such images are being used for illustrative purposes only.
Certain stock imagery © Getty Images.

Interior Image Credit: Christa Craycraft
Title Script Artist: Kestrel Montes

"Scripture quotations are from the ESV® Bible (The Holy Bible, English Standard Version®), copyright © 2001 by Crossway, a publishing ministry of Good News Publishers. Used by permission. All rights reserved."

ISBN: 978-1-6642-4431-3 (sc)
ISBN: 978-1-6642-4433-7 (hc)
ISBN: 978-1-6642-4432-0 (e)

Library of Congress Control Number: 2021918309

Print information available on the last page.

WestBow Press rev. date: 09/15/2021

WESTBOW
PRESS®
A DIVISION OF THOMAS NELSON
& ZONDERVAN

Dear NICU Parent,

As you embark on this NICU journey with your child, there will likely be times where you may feel overwhelmed with every single emotion, and times where you may feel numb to all of them. When they tell you it will be a roller coaster ride, buckle up, because they're not lying. However, you WILL get through this.

I pray this book will help to create a moment where you can escape all the complexities of the situation to feel only the overwhelming love between you and your baby. I hope that you will find a moment like this in each and every day you spend together. I won't promise you that all the other emotions won't return; however, I promise that once you find a way to see beyond the medical aspects and focus on the love, you will find a strength you didn't know you had. There will likely be times where you will feel broken, tired, and weak; during those times, you will find grace to make it yet another day.

When your NICU journey comes to an end, you will likely look back and question how in the world you made it through; the answer will be LOVE. After all,

"Love bears all things, believes all things, hopes all things, endures all things. Love never fails." 1 Corinthians 13:7 ESV

Sincerely,
Melissa (former NICU mom)

Hello, little love! We are so glad you're here!

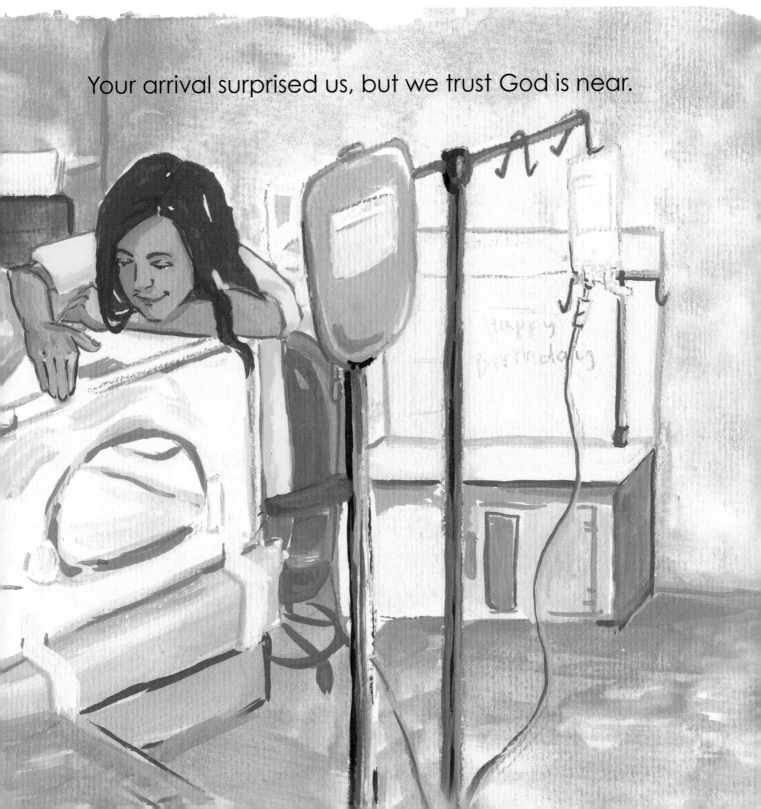

Your arrival surprised us, but we trust God is near.

We want you to know
you are loved beyond measure,

and each moment we share
is considered a treasure.

As you lay sleeping we count all your toes,

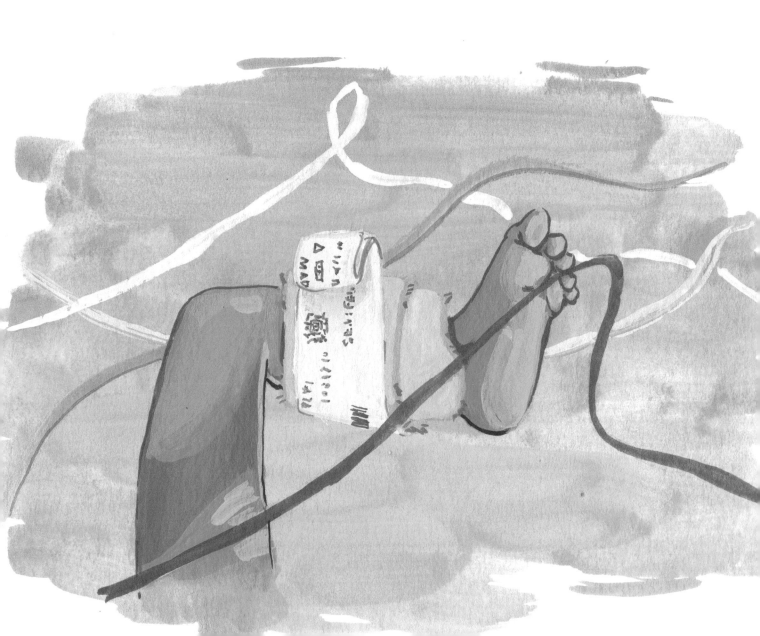

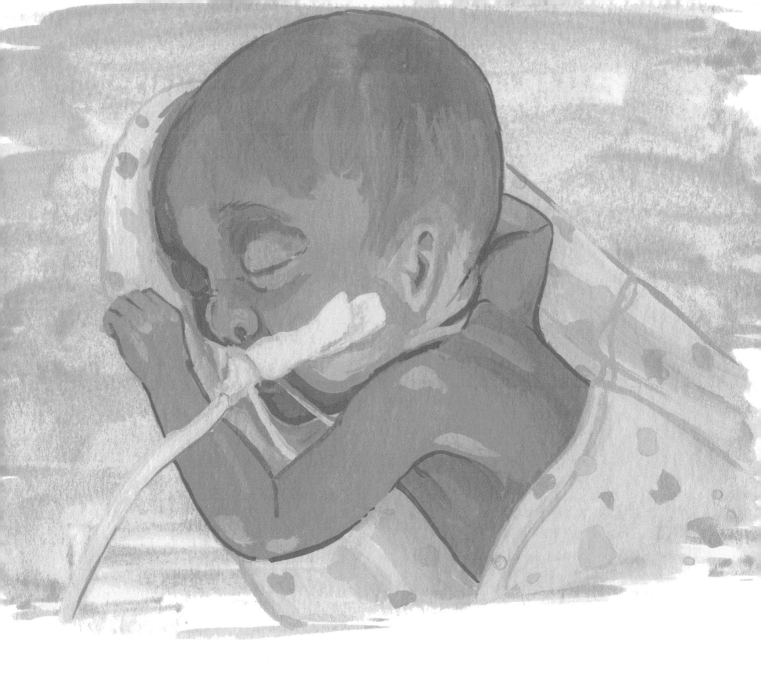

and gaze at your tiny-but-*perfect*-shaped nose.

When we soak in your details, so *wonderfully* made,

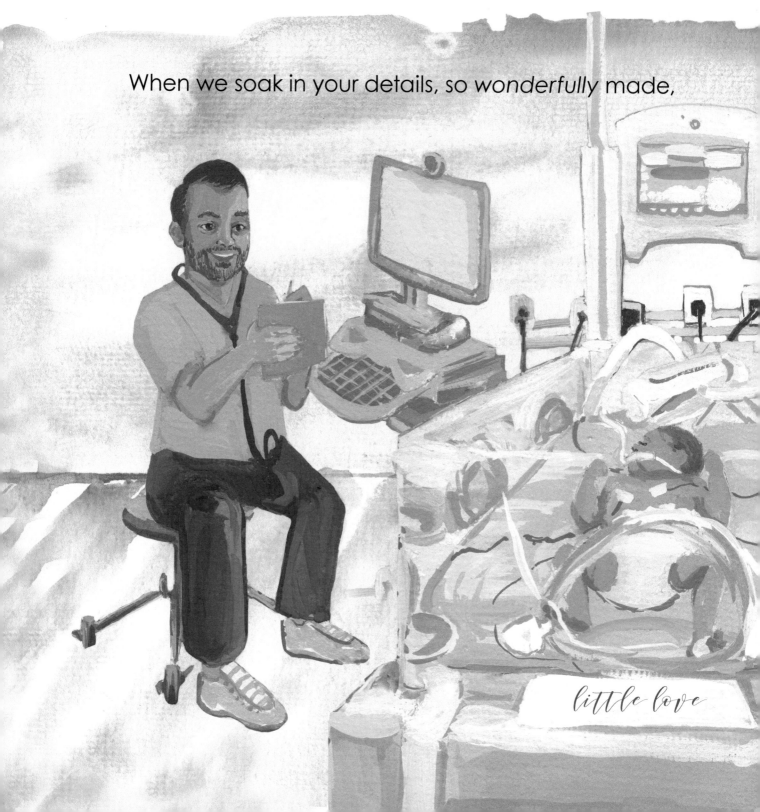

*little love*

your

wires,

and

beeping,

and

problems

*all*

f a d e.

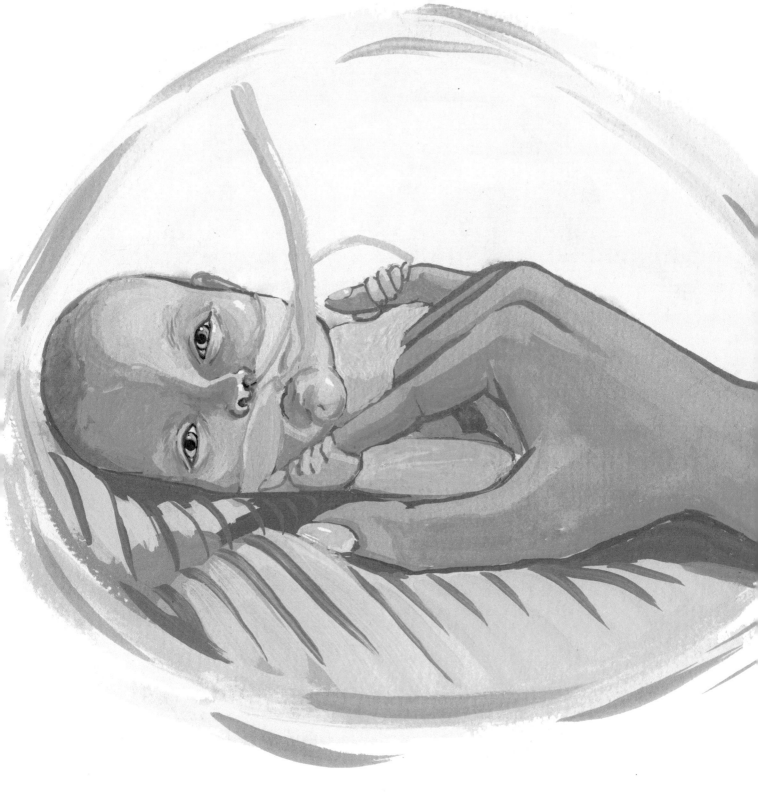

That is when we really see
Y O U.

You are tiny but
S T R O N G

You are fragile yet
R E S I L I E N T.

You are B R A V E.
You are L O V E D.
You are O U R S.

It's a blessing to know you

and despite all our fear,

you are worth

every prayer,

each worry,

and tear.

As we watch you grow,

our faith grows, too!

God gave us a gift,

When He gave us

Y O U.

The following pages may be used to journal to your own little love!

# **Hello!**

My name is

_____

Date _____

Weight_____

Length _____

Time _____

Dear _____,

_____

_____

_____

_____

_____

_____

_____

_____

_____

_____

_____

_____

Love,

# About the Author

Melissa and her husband, Chris reside in NE Ohio with their three earth side children, Asher, Cora, and Jane, and are awaiting a sweet heavenly reunion with their firstborn, Audrey. Melissa is a former NICU mother to 3 micro-preemies. She currently stays home to care for her children. Melissa has used journaling as a way to process, understand, and heal from the trauma that accompanies prematurity. As a result of her journaling, "Hello, Little Love!" was born. Melissa hopes to use her own experiences to help others walking through a similar journey.

Printed in the United States
by Baker & Taylor Publisher Services